T0011181

WHAT YOU NEVER KNEW ABOUT

DWAYNE
JOHNSON

by Mari Schuh

CAPSTONE PRESS
a capstone imprint

For Matt at Brick Street Market & Café in Bondurant, Iowa

This is an unauthorized biography.

Spark is published by Capstone Press, an imprint of Capstone
1710 Roe Crest Drive, North Mankato, Minnesota 56003
capstonepub.com

Library of Congress Cataloging-in-Publication Data is available on the Library of Congress website.
ISBN: 9781669002970 (hardcover)
ISBN: 9781669040552 (paperback)
ISBN: 9781669002932 (ebook PDF)

Summary: Young readers learn behind-the-scenes facts and exciting details about actor and pro wrestler Dwayne "The Rock" Johnson.

Editorial Credits
Editor: Erika L. Shores; Designer: Heidi Thompson; Media Researcher: Jo Miller; Production Specialist: Tori Abraham

Image Credits
Alamy: Everett Collection, Inc., 15, WENN Rights Ltd, 28; Avalon: face to face, 25, Photoshot, 8; Getty Images: Andreas Rentz, 26, Newspix, 4, Rob Carr, 23; Newscom: Alberto Reyes/WENN.com, 14, MAVRIXONLINE.COM, 21, Octavio Jones/Tampa Bay Times via ZUMA Wire, 19; Shutterstock: Africa Studio, 9, Alexander Raths, 22, CloudyStock, 11 (top), Cubankite, 7, DFree, 13, Featureflash Photo Agency, 16, Kathy Hutchins, 18, Mark_KA, 24, Nikita Konashenkov, 6, okansurmen, 20, OriIfergan, 11 (bottom), Sterling Munksgard, 10, timquo, 27, Tinseltown, cover, 29

All internet sites appearing in back matter were available and accurate when this book was sent to press.

TABLE OF CONTENTS

Words in **bold** are in the glossary.

MEGASTAR

We'll get your body f

Dwayne "The Rock" Johnson is a **megastar** known around the world. So how does The Rock stay in shape when he's away from home making movies? He brings a gym with him! It takes semitrucks and hundreds of people to set up the traveling gym.

What else might surprise you about Dwayne? It's time to find out!

DID YOU KNOW?

Think you're a superfan? Did you know:

- **Dwayne has many nicknames. He is called The Rock, La Roca, and The Great One. He is also called The People's Champion and DJ.**

- **He seems outgoing, but he can be shy.**

- **He takes three showers a day.**

- **He owns a life-size model of a T. Rex skull.**

The **tattoo** on Dwayne's right arm is full of meaning. Cracks in the skull stand for hard lessons he has learned. The horns point straight ahead. That means moving forward to the next goal. The eye is a symbol of being positive.

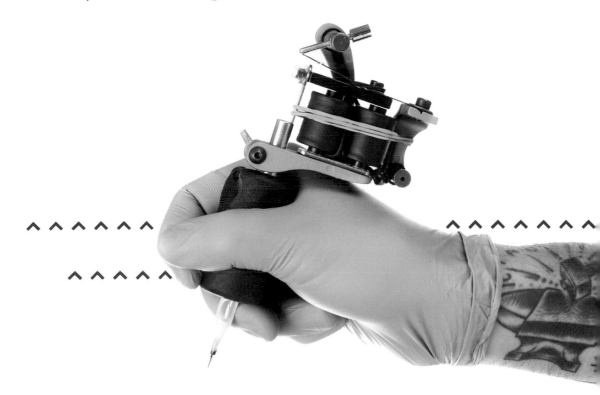

Dwayne loves wrestling and acting. But he also loves music. He plays the guitar and the **ukulele**. Willie Nelson is one of his favorite singers.

Willie Nelson

The Rock's biggest loves are his wife and three daughters. He calls his youngest two daughters tornadoes. They have lots of energy! He takes them fishing. He paints their nails. They have tea parties too.

DJ'S FAVES

Have you been keeping up with The Rock?

How many of his favorite things do you know?

1. Favorite vehicle?

2. Favorite food made by his mom?

3. Favorite sport moments?

4. Favorite movies?

5. Bonus point for Dwayne's favorite thing about being famous!

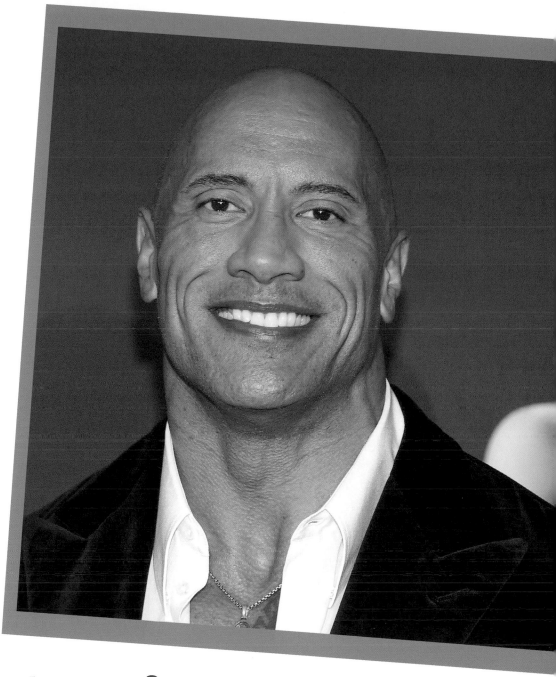

1. Pickup truck **2.** Samoan chow mein

3. Winning the football national championship for the University of Miami Hurricanes and headlining five WrestleManias

4. *Jurassic Park* and *It's a Wonderful Life* **5.** Making people happy

13

DWAYNE BY THE NUMBERS

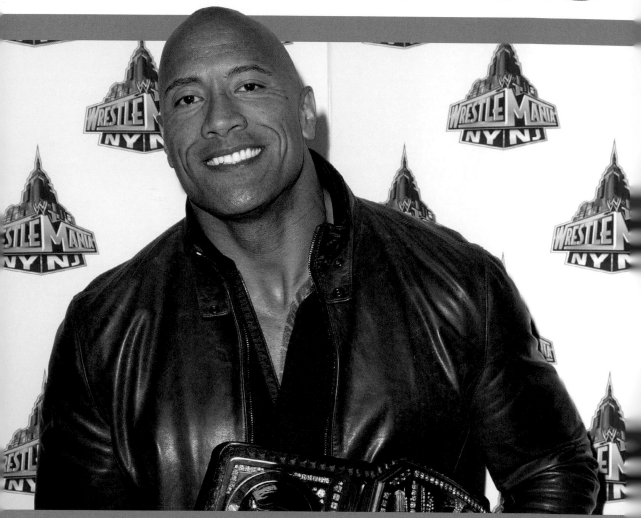

Dwayne was born May 2, 1972. He won 10 world titles as a pro wrestler. As a movie star, his movies have brought in more than $10 billion around the world. Ka-ching!

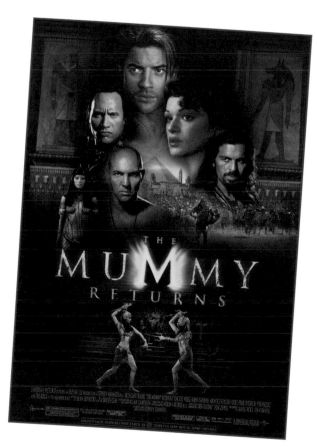

10,000,000,000

332,0

✗ ✗ ✗ ✗ ✗ ✗ ✗ ✗ ✗ ✗ ✗ ✗ ✗ ✗ ✗

At 6 feet, 5 inches tall, Dwayne is large and in charge. His social media numbers are huge too. He has more than 332 million Instagram followers. At least 16.3 million people follow him on Twitter.

✗ ✗ ✗ ✗ ✗ ✗ ✗

LITTLE **ROCK**

Dwayne isn't the only pro wrestler in his family. His grandpa and his dad, Rocky Johnson, were famous wrestlers too.

Dwayne's family moved a lot when he was young. When he was in kindergarten, he had already lived in five states.

SENSATIONAL SUPER STAR

ARRIVES IN FLORIDA

ROCKY JOHNSON

FACT

By age 13, Dwayne had lived in 13 different states.

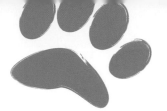

Dwayne had a dog when he was growing up. But they didn't just go for walks. He practiced wrestling moves on his pup!

FEAST MODE

Wanna know what The Rock is cooking? His big body needs big meals. He eats 10 pounds of food a day. He chows on fish, eggs, and vegetables. He usually eats one or two steaks a day.

On Sundays, Dwayne eats whatever he wants. He enjoys French toast that he calls Rock Toast. One Sunday meal in 2012 was huge. He ate 21 brownies, 4 pizzas, and 12 pancakes.

ROCKIN' THE SELFIE

The Rock was the king of **selfies** in 2015. Flashing his huge smile, he set a world record for taking selfies. In just three minutes, he took photos with 105 fans. Now that's fast and furious!

FACT

In 2022, Dwayne introduced the teams playing in the Super Bowl.

THE PEOPLE'S
CHAMPION

Dwayne loves his pickup trucks.

He also loves his fans. Dwayne gave a

lucky fan one of his own pickup trucks.

No wonder he's called The Great One!

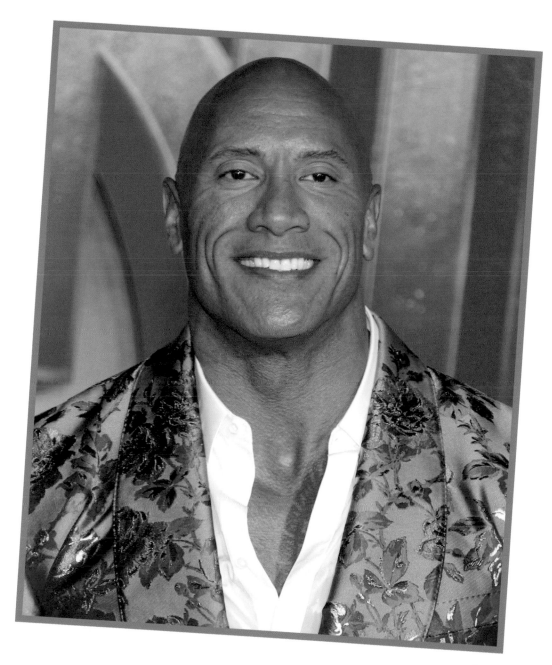

"...Kindness matters. It matters."

–Dwayne Johnson

Glossary

megastar (MEG-uh-star)—a person who is very famous

selfie (SELL-fee)—a photo you take of yourself with your smartphone, usually to post on social media

tattoo (ta-TOO)—a picture that has been printed onto a person's skin with pigments and needles

ukulele (you-kah-LAY-lee)—a small musical instrument that has four strings

Read More

Abdo, Kenny. *Dwayne Johnson*. Minneapolis: Fly! An Imprint of Abdo Zoom, 2019.

Rose, Rachel. *Dwayne Johnson: Actor and Pro Wrestler*. Minneapolis: Bearport Publishing Company, 2022.

Santos, Rita. *Dwayne "The Rock" Johnson: Pro Wrestler and Actor*. New York: Enslow Publishing, 2020.

Internet Sites

10 Things You May Not Know About Dwayne "The Rock" Johnson
biography.com/news/dwayne-johnson-the-rock-facts

35 Interesting Facts About Dwayne Johnson
thefactsite.com/dwayne-johnson-facts/

Dwayne "The Rock" Johnson
wwe.com/superstars/the-rock

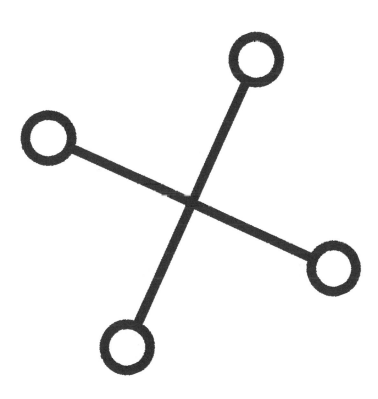

Index

About the Author

Mari Schuh's love of reading began with cereal boxes at the kitchen table. Today she is the author of hundreds of nonfiction books for young readers. Mari lives in the Midwest with her husband and their sassy house rabbit. Learn more about her at marischuh.com.